# THE
# **STRENGTHS**
# WORKBOOK

## SALLY BIBB

AN EIGHT-WEEK PROGRAMME TO
DISCOVER YOUR STRENGTHS AND
WHAT MAKES YOU THRIVE

Published by
**LID Publishing Limited**
The Record Hall, Studio 204,
16-16a Baldwins Gardens,
London EC1N 7RJ, UK

info@lidpublishing.com
www.lidpublishing.com

A member of:

www.businesspublishersroundtable.com

© Sally Bibb, 2019
© LID Publishing Limited, 2019
Reprinted in 2019

Printed in Latvia by Jelgavas Tipогrāfij

ISBN: 978-1-912555-38-3

Cover and page design: Matthew Renaudin

# THE
# **STRENGTHS**
# WORKBOOK

## SALLY BIBB

AN EIGHT-WEEK PROGRAMME TO
DISCOVER YOUR STRENGTHS AND
WHAT MAKES YOU THRIVE

MADRID | MEXICO CITY | LONDON
NEW YORK | BUENOS AIRES
BOGOTA | SHANGHAI | NEW DELHI

# CONTENTS

# WHAT YOU'LL GET FROM *THE STRENGTHS WORKBOOK*

*The Strengths Workbook* is an eight-week programme that you can start any time. You will identify your innate strengths, values and motivations, and discover how you can further develop them and use them to your advantage.

When you understand yourself in this way, you know what will make you fulfilled, happy and successful. It means you can become the best version of yourself, as well as build your self-confidence about who you are.

This workbook is for you if you want to make choices that are right for you and become more energized, fulfilled and effective in your life, work or relationships.

## DO YOU NEED
## *THE STRENGTHS WORKBOOK?*

Would you like to:

- Feel more fulfilled?
- Achieve your goals more easily?
- Feel more confident?
- Be energized and motivated?
- Stay on track?
- Overcome obstacles?

If you've answered 'yes' to any of these questions, *The Strengths Workbook* eight-week programme will help you. It's simple and practical, and will help you discover and develop your strengths and lead a more fulfilled life.

## WHAT CAN *THE STRENGTHS WORKBOOK* DO FOR YOU?

There are numerous reasons for using *The Strengths Workbook*. You may want to be sure that you're choosing a course of study or a career path in which you'll be happy and thrive. Or, if you're discontented in your current job or career, you can use the workbook to help you identify something you truly love doing.

# HOW TO USE
# *THE STRENGTHS*
# *WORKBOOK*

As you work through the workbook, it's most useful if you focus on a particular area of your life or work. It might be a project you're involved in, you might be about to start a new job or you might be experiencing a stressful situation and wondering how you can help yourself through it.

Alternatively, you may have a particular goal you want to achieve. Complete the next page and write down what your area of focus will be before you get started.

- **Name:**

- **Contact details to return this book if lost:**

- **What I want from the workbook**
  **(write down your area of focus or goal):**

This workbook is based on an eight-week programme and sticking to it is the best way to get the most from it. However, we're all busy, so if you miss a day, don't worry, just pick up where you've left off. The best way is to set aside 15–20 minutes each day to dedicate to working through the exercises.

**It works like this:**
Every week you have a number of exercises to complete. These exercises can be broken down into three parts:

1. At the beginning of each week, you'll be asked to complete a simple exercise to help you gain insight into some aspect of what makes you tick.
2. Throughout the week, you'll answer some questions that will help you reflect and learn more about yourself.
3. At the end of each week, you'll be asked to look back on your week and review what you've learned.

After working through each week, you'll find a short story that is an example of how the insight from this programme can lead to a richer, fuller work or personal life. Finally, each week ends with a takeaway tip to help you apply that week's lesson to your everyday life.

## HOW TO LEARN MORE
## ABOUT STRENGTHS

To learn more about strengths and how you can use and develop them, check out *The Strengths Book: Discover How to Be Fulfilled in Your Work and In Life*, also by Sally Bibb, which gives more background on strengths and some additional exercises. It's an excellent companion to *The Strengths Workbook*.

# WHAT ARE STRENGTHS AND WHY ARE THEY IMPORTANT?

We spend about a third of our lives working.

Yet only 13% of workers worldwide are happy at work. More than half of the UK's workers say they are in the wrong career.

This is a sad situation and one of the reasons *The Strengths Workbook* is useful. It's to help more people get into work they love.

When you're playing to your strengths in your work, you're fulfilled and perform better because work doesn't feel like too much effort. It energizes you and you enjoy your days. This is in stark contrast to not playing to your natural strengths in your work. If you're trying to be something you're not, you become unhappy, your confidence drops and your overall wellbeing can become badly affected quickly.

Aside from your work life, participating in hobbies, studies and relationships where you can be who you are, where you can express your true self and use your strengths is important for happiness and wellbeing.

# WHAT IS A STRENGTH?

A strength is something that someone is naturally good at, loves doing and is energized by.

Our strengths are innate. They are developed by the time we reach our mid-teens. By then, we are who we are. While we can continue to learn new skills or acquire new knowledge throughout our lives, what we are like as a person doesn't fundamentally change.

An example of an innate strength is connecting with other people. Have you ever noticed how great baristas in coffee shops do this? They can't help it. They can't *not* do it. Another example is the athlete who is naturally competitive. They just have to win. It's part of who they are.

Think of your strengths as something you can't *not* do. These are the things that feel like a natural part of who you are. Take a moment to think about what that means to you. What sorts of things do you naturally do? Do you almost always:

- Talk to people in lifts, queues or on trains?
- Have a list of things to do, even on weekends?
- Strive to always finish first?
- See problems that need solving?

If you said a big 'yes, that's me!' to any of these things, it's an indication that it's one of your strengths.

Using our strengths energizes us. If you answered 'no' to any of the things above, chances are it's because it's not one of your natural strengths. These are the things you would probably avoid doing, and if you did them they would drain you.

**Your strengths reflect the real you.**
**You can't NOT be this way.**

This workbook also looks at your proud moments, motivations, values, overdone strengths and weaknesses, because they all form part of the picture of who you are and why you are that way. This self-knowledge is important if you're to make deliberate choices about how you live your life and the work you choose to do.

## WHY ARE STRENGTHS IMPORTANT?

Have you ever felt like you were trying to be something you're not? Or that you were doing a job where you were expected to be someone you're not?

The reason for these feelings may have been that you were doing things you weren't cut out for. This is what happened to me when I was promoted into a job involving hours working on spreadsheets. I learned the knowledge and skills to be good enough to perform that role, but I lacked the excitement for numbers and data, and I was never going to love it.

So it is important that you are doing things that make use of your strengths.

Our strengths are important because:

- They are the real us. What's the point of going against the grain of who we are, when we can thrive by being truer to who we are?
- They build our confidence. This is because they are us at our best – they're the things we're naturally good at.
- We can let go of the idea that we *should* be different in some way.

The big thing about using our strengths is that then we get to live *our* life and not somebody else's!

———

## OUR STRENGTHS DRIVE OUR BEHAVIOUR

Think of your strengths as the deepest part of you. They are the engine that drives how you act. For example, if you're a person who loves to take responsibility, this will show itself in behaviours like offering to take on projects, making that important phone call that no one else wants to make, and just getting on and doing the things that need doing.

Our strengths can also lead us to behave in a way that is uncomfortable or unnatural. For example, if you're not an assertive person but doing the right thing is really important to you, there are times when you may need to be assertive despite shaking inside.

I witnessed this very thing when I saw a nurse standing up to a doctor. She wasn't a naturally assertive person. She wouldn't be the sort of person who would send an unsatisfactory meal back in a restaurant, but that is because the meal wouldn't matter that much to her. But when a doctor was compromising her patients' wellbeing by his actions, she stood up to him even though she felt intimidated and nervous. Two of her strengths (doing the right thing and having high standards) resulted in a behaviour that was not her natural way of being.

---

## OUTDATED IDEAS TO LET GO OF

**You should be a well-rounded person**
Much of our school and work life is designed around making us well-rounded people. We are expected to reach good grades in all our subjects and to achieve good standards of performance in our company's required list of competences.

This is unrealistic and undesirable. Imagine if Andy Murray, world class tennis player, had tried to be good at all his school subjects. He probably would have been unhappier and much less proficient at sports because a lot of his energy would have been used up on things he didn't really like and was never going to be good at.

None of us can be good at everything. If we spend time and energy trying to be good at everything, we will become mediocre at many things and not great at anything.

## You don't have enough strengths and need to develop more

The idea that some people are lacking strengths is incorrect. We all have strengths – the problem is most people either don't know their strengths, take them for granted or are unsure how to use them to their best advantage.

As you work through this programme, you will discover a set of strengths that, if put to work, will make you happy and great at what you do.

## Excellent performance comes from fixing our weaknesses

The – probably unconscious – assumption in organizations is that to achieve excellence, weaknesses have to be eradicated. Many, if not most, employers take their people's strengths for granted and focus on getting them to fix their weaknesses. This leads to mediocre performance at best. It certainly doesn't result in motivated, confident workers.

It also means that most of an organization's training budget is spent on trying to fix weaknesses rather than on developing people to improve in their areas of strength. Or, even better, it could be spent on putting the resources into selecting people into roles where they will be a great fit in the first place.

### You need to be different to be better

For most of us, the exact opposite is true. **You actually need to be more of who you *really* are, deep down, to be better.** Sure, you might need to learn new skills or knowledge to add to the raw materials of 'you', but if you keep trying to be different, you will always be frustrated.

People don't have to change in order to be excellent. They just have to understand who they are and what their innate strengths are. They then must work on those things like crazy until they reach excellence.

An example is René Carayol, the broadcaster and speaker. One of his strengths is his passion. Early in his career in a big retail company, he was repeatedly asked to 'tone it down'. That was a ridiculous notion, as it is one of his great strengths. In his current work, his passion plus his knowledge and skill of being able to tell a good story make him an exciting and engaging speaker.

René is a great example of someone who knows and uses his strengths to achieve success and happiness. If he'd stayed in his old job, he would have felt dampened by the fact that his company wanted him to be different.

**It's unrealistic to expect to enjoy your job**
The idea of just getting on and putting up with work we
don't enjoy is deep-rooted. It's likely that it originates from
an era where a lot of people worked in awful jobs and
harsh conditions, a time when work was simply a matter of
survival and not an opportunity for self-expression.

Nowadays it's reasonable to expect to get something out of
work other than a mere wage. If you know what makes you
tick, you can find fulfilment in work.

**Progressing means climbing the career ladder**
It's been an unchallenged assumption for years that
progressing means moving upwards in an organization's
hierarchy. Do you know anyone who was promoted from a
job in which they were happy to a managerial role, only to
realize they didn't like managing and weren't very good at
it? This is quite common.

However, since Generation Y (otherwise known as the
'Millennials') entered the workforce, that notion has been
challenged. Generation Y is less inclined to think of pro-
gression as vertical than as horizontal growth. They are
more concerned with the notion of 'fit'. That's a great question to always keep in mind – is this a good fit?

This different way of thinking can be hard for people to
get used to because it's not a common practice. But it is
common sense. I had a conversation with a nurse who,
while she hadn't thought about it too much, had always

assumed that her next career move would be a rung up the ladder to be a ward sister. What she discovered was that she loves being a nurse. She loves the day-to-day contact with patients, and she actually doesn't like being in charge. During our discussion, she realized that she would be a round peg in a square hole as a ward sister. Far from being disappointed, she was relieved to have realized this when she did.

### Having a career is superior to having a job

The idea of a career being superior to a job is probably to do with notions of personal fulfilment, satisfaction, contribution to society and achievement of potential. Parents often feel their children are not fulfilling their potential if they choose one job when they could do 'so much better'. A job is often thought of as something someone simply does for the money rather than to gain any intrinsic satisfaction from it. There is certainly more status attached to 'having a career' than there is to 'having a job'.

This thinking is challenged by the strengths movement, which focuses on the route to satisfaction instead of thinking about jobs versus careers. Working in a call centre could be considered 'just a job', as could working in a coffee shop or as a delivery driver. But my colleagues and I at my company, Engaging Minds, have actually discovered, in our work with many people in all sorts of organizations, that there are people in all of the aforementioned roles who love their jobs and say things like 'I can't believe I get paid to do this'.

My point is, all individuals have their own unique set of strengths. So, it makes no difference whether you call your work a job or career. What matters is that you love what you do every day.

## Positive thinking leads to happiness

The positive thinking movement encourages people to be positive even when they're not feeling positive. The movement asserts that in order to be happy, you need to think positively.

However, research shows that trying to think positively won't make you happy. If we try and push emotions like sadness, grief and anger to one side, we actually become less happy. Happiness is a by-product of doing things that we find intrinsically valuable. It's not a state you can achieve by just changing your thoughts.

So, if you're unhappy at work, school, college or in your relationship, thinking positively won't change that. In fact, it may make it worse, because you feel you ought to be able to think yourself into a positive frame of mind.

# HOW ARE STRENGTHS FORMED?

Our strengths are created by synapses in the brain. A synapse is a connection between two brain cells that enables the cells (neurons) to communicate with one another. Crudely speaking, your synapses create your strengths.

On day 42 after conception, your brain creates its first neuron, and 120 days later you have 100 billion – creating 9,500 neurons every second. Sixty days before you are born, your neurons start to communicate with each other and make connections (synapses).

By age three, each of your 100 billion neurons will have formed 15,000 synaptic connections with other neurons. That's 15,000 connections for each of your 100 billion neurons.

But then things take a strange turn. Nature now prompts you to ignore a lot of your woven connections and as these get neglected, they fall into disuse and connections start to break. Between the ages of three and 15, you lose billions of these synaptic connections.

By age 16½, the network is essentially gone. And you can't rebuild it. Your genetic inheritance and early childhood experiences assist you in finding some connections smoother and easier to use than others (e.g. the caring connections or the strategic or relating connections). Through use or nurture, some of these dwindle while others are used and honed so that they become very well established.

By puberty, these synaptic connections are formed and after that, we don't really change that much.

Think of it this way: our strengths are like a four-lane superhighway of the brain – the connections that are fast and efficient are those that are used often and are well trodden. The connections (or synapses) that are used less often are like a minor road that is unfamiliar, more difficult to navigate and not an enjoyable experience.

---

## DO STRENGTHS CHANGE?

Our strengths don't change, because they are an intrinsic part of who we are. They might get stronger with use. Or they may fade if we don't use them. But they are always there.

We can change our behaviour, but what thrills us or drains us stays fairly constant over time. For example, if you are a very competitive person, you can't help but compare your performance with other people's.

What CAN you change about yourself?

Ok, so we've established that we can't (and shouldn't try to) change who we fundamentally are, i.e. our strengths.

So what can we change?

- We can learn new skills.
- We can acquire new knowledge.
- We can (to some extent) change our behaviour.

For example, if you become a manager, you should already have that important raw ingredient of a great manager – you love to be in charge or to lead others. But you may have no idea how to give feedback or run a team meeting. These are skills you can learn.

You may need to know something about employment law. This is knowledge you can acquire by reading or taking courses.

You may have been told that you sometimes get carried away and talk too fast and lose people. Well, you can modify that behaviour and slow down your speech, for example, when you are explaining something complex.

# WHAT ABOUT WEAKNESSES?

Some employers use the euphemism 'areas for development' instead of 'weaknesses'. I can see why. They are trying to make weaknesses feel less negative. But weaknesses are not negative. Every one of us has weaknesses, just like every one of us has strengths. It's part of being human.

We need not be ashamed of our weaknesses. It's better to accept that we have them and then decide whether we want to do something about them.

But before we get on to that, it's helpful to split weaknesses into two types: those that matter and those that don't. Most of our weaknesses are irrelevant because they don't get in the way of us performing well in what we choose to do.

For example, if you're a journalist and you're not very good at physically fixing things, it doesn't matter. But a journalist who isn't good at clearly communicating wouldn't be a very good journalist.

So, focus only on the weaknesses that matter.

When we concentrate on our strengths rather than dwelling on our weaknesses, we can start to achieve our full potential.

## What about the other elements covered in this programme?

You'll notice that this workbook also contains sections on proud moments, motivations, values, strengths on overdrive, weaknesses and influences. It's because they are all related to bringing out the best in ourselves: our motivations and our values are part of our strengths; we need to be able to identify when we're on overdrive with our strengths because that can hinder us; we need to know our weaknesses and how to work with or around them; and we also need to understand how we are influenced, so that we are empowered to be in control of our reactions.

Don't worry about these labels, though. The important thing is that you do the exercises for each week. One by one, you'll get insight that helps you achieve what you want and be who you really are.

Are you ready to get started?

**To make a start, have a go at this exercise.**

| Strengths | Very much like me | A bit like me | Not very much like me |
|---|---|---|---|
| I love to be in charge<br>*I'm naturally drawn to take the lead in any situation* | | | |
| I'm a very competitive person<br>*It's very important for me to be the best* | | | |
| I have a lot of drive<br>*I'm not satisfied until I have achieved what I set out to do* | | | |
| I keep going when things are tough<br>*I'm energized by overcoming obstacles and setbacks* | | | |
| I bring energy and pace to everything I do<br>*I get a lot done, fast* | | | |
| It's very important to me to do the right thing<br>*I'm the type of person who speaks up or takes risks if something is not right* | | | |
| I'm honest and straightforward<br>*People know where they stand with me* | | | |
| I'm naturally optimistic<br>*I usually assume that things will turn out well* | | | |
| I believe in myself<br>*I'm usually confident that I can make a positive contribution* | | | |
| I get a buzz out of learning<br>*I continuously look for opportunities to develop and grow* | | | |
| I love developing others<br>*I get great satisfaction from watching others progress and realize their potential* | | | |

| Strengths | Very much like me | A bit like me | Not very much like me |
|---|---|---|---|
| **I instinctively tune in to other people's needs** <br> *I realize if something is wrong with someone and I'm good at understanding situations from other peoples' perspectives* | | | |
| **I care about people** <br> *Others' wellbeing is really important to me* | | | |
| **I love to think about the big picture** <br> *I'm good at understanding how things connect* | | | |
| **I have a restless desire to improve things** <br> *I'm always searching for ways to do things better or more efficiently* | | | |
| **I'm good at explaining things** <br> *I communicate information in ways that others find easy to understand* | | | |
| **I love making connections** <br> *I enjoy bringing people together for their mutual benefit* | | | |
| **I love making decisions** <br> *I thrive on weighing the options and selecting the best way forward* | | | |
| **I intuitively know what's really important** <br> *I find it easy to figure out and focus my attention on the things that count* | | | |
| **I'm good at analysing data and situations** <br> *I enjoy the challenge of making sense of complex and sometimes incomplete information* | | | |

| Strengths | Very much like me | A bit like me | Not very much like me |
|---|---|---|---|
| **I'm always coming up with new ways of doing things**<br>*Creative thinking comes naturally to me* | | | |
| **I thrive on solving problems**<br>*I enjoy the challenge of finding solutions to issues and challenges* | | | |
| **I have very high standards**<br>*I strive to achieve excellence* | | | |
| **I love to work with my hands**<br>*I get a buzz from doing practical tasks* | | | |
| **I'm good at adapting to changing situations**<br>*I quickly and easily juggle priorities and resources to meet unexpected demands* | | | |
| **I'm energized by working with other people**<br>*I love collaborating and being part of a team* | | | |
| **I love to bring a smile to others' faces**<br>*I'm good at seeing and sharing the funny side of things* | | | |
| **I thrive on personal responsibility**<br>*I take pride in always doing what I say I'll do* | | | |
| **I'm disciplined**<br>*I love to organize things so I achieve my deadlines* | | | |
| **I'm a very positive person**<br>*I tend to see the upside of things and people* | | | |

Which of the strengths did you mark as 'very much like me' and out of those, which do you think are the MOST like you?

**Write them down on the next page.**

This isn't a definitive list, so if any other strengths come to mind that are not on the list, add those too.

# MY TOP STRENGTHS

# CONFIRM YOUR STRENGTHS

To double-check that these really are your true strengths, ask yourself these questions in relation to each of your strengths.

## Enthusiasm

1. Do you mostly look forward to doing or being *(insert name of strength)*?
2. Do you get a buzz out of it?
3. Is it something that you don't tend to put off doing?
4. Does it feel like not much of an effort?
5. Would you volunteer to use this strength/do this activity more if you could?

## Success

6. Do you think you're good at it?
7. Have other people commented that you're good at it?
8. Have you been given praise or recognition for this strength or what you have achieved as a result of using it?

## Ease

9. Does this come fairly easy to you?
10. Sometimes do you wonder why others find it much harder to do than you do?
11. Have you always been this way?
12. Does this feel natural to you?

If you've answered 'yes' to most of these questions, then the likelihood is that the strength in question is indeed one of your strengths. There is no 'correct score'. Having gone through these questions, use your instinct or gut reaction to gauge whether this is part of the real you.

**We're going to come back to your strengths in Week 2 because there is more to discover!**

**THE**

# EIGHT-WEEK

**PROGRAMME**

# WEEK 1

# PROUD
# MOMENTS

"THE GREAT THING
ABOUT KNOWING
YOUR STRENGTHS
IS YOU GET TO
LIVE YOUR OWN
LIFE AND NOT
SOMEONE ELSE'S."

SALLY BIBB

# PROUD MOMENTS

A proud moment is a time when you feel particularly pleased with what you have done. The reason it's good to remember such moments is because it's inspiring and positive to do so. Also, it's likely that the times you're proud are the times you're also playing to your strengths. For example, if you made an effort to go to a friend's birthday party when you didn't feel like it, that could be because you're a caring person who puts themselves out for others.

Proud moments can also be times when you've stretched yourself. Perhaps you've done something that was scary or required you to take a risk. For example, if you did a talk despite being extremely nervous of public speaking. What was it that made you do it anyway? Was it that you cared about getting your story out there more than you were worried about not performing well? In that case, maybe you're a courageous person who wants to make a difference.

You can also be proud of recognition or accolades. It pays to reflect on these times, as it can give you insight into yourself. Whether it's a major prize or a simple thank you from someone, think about why you were given that recognition. Was it that you persevered against the odds, showed yourself to be a very caring person or perhaps went the extra mile? Whatever it was that led you to be appreciated, think about it, because that's a window into understanding yourself more too.

## EXERCISE

1

Think about things you've done so far in your life that you're proud of. They don't have to be big things or major achievements. They can be as simple as if you were kind to the lonely next-door neighbour or you kept going in difficult circumstances.

As you think of things this week, make a note of them here.

**EXERCISE**

## End-of-week reflection:

Read through all the things you're
proud of. What is it about you that
made you do those things? Read
the introduction to this week to help
prompt your thinking.

Make a note here of what your proud
moments reveal about the kind of
person you are.

# SONIA'S STORY

Sonia didn't do well at school, but she worked hard in her first job and became a respected secretary. She married young and was happy for 20 years. One day her husband announced he was leaving. She hadn't seen it coming and was devastated. One thing she says she's extremely proud of is how she coped in those dark days. She turned to family and friends and didn't become bitter. After a while, she took up some new hobbies, one of which gave her the opportunity to travel. She said she wouldn't have considered travelling alone until then.

The strengths that Sonia says most of her proud moments show are that she's a loyal person who also has loyal friends and family, she's determined and resilient, and she is also a curious person which means she will try things even if she feels nervous.

## HOW IS THIS WEEK'S INSIGHT GOING TO HELP YOU?

In a few ways:

- If you're not feeling great about yourself, remembering your proudest moments will give you a boost and remind you of some real positives that you can be pleased with.
- Being conscious of the positive things about yourself helps you to bring those things to bear more often.
- Having a good idea of what you're proud of and do well can help you to stretch and develop yourself further. For example, if you realize you're courageous, then challenge yourself to do things that you're afraid of doing but which you want to do.

# TIP

If you're feeling modest and find that you are underplaying your proud moments, imagine that you are your best friend. It's easier for us to tell others how proud we are of them than it is to do that for ourselves.

# NOTES

**WEEK 2**

STRENGTHS

"EVERYONE IS A GENIUS.
BUT IF YOU JUDGE A FISH
ON ITS ABILITY TO CLIMB
A TREE, IT WILL LIVE ITS
WHOLE LIFE BELIEVING
IT IS STUPID."

ALBERT EINSTEIN

# STRENGTHS

When people become clear about their strengths, it makes them more motivated, confident and settled just because of that knowledge. Knowing our strengths allows us to understand more clearly why we are happy in certain situations and not in others.

The exercise on **page 23** and those for this week will help you get a really good idea of what your strengths are.

As we've already learned, things that we love doing, are good at and are energized by are usually our strengths. This week's exercises will help you to start identifying these things.

At the beginning of the week,
think about and answer the
following questions.

- **What do I love doing?**
  *Example: "Sitting with an elderly neighbour to give his son a break"*

## What makes me enjoy this?
*"I love helping people and I enjoy hearing their life stories"*

## What's it like when I'm doing this?
*"It makes me feel valued and it's a worthwhile thing to do"*

- **What gives me a buzz?**
  *Example: "Negotiating contracts"*

What makes me enjoy this?
*"I love being analytical and I get a buzz out of influencing people"*

What's it like when I'm doing this?
*"It's satisfying when we reach an agreement"*

- **What never feels like hard work to me?**
  *Example: "Filing, chatting with people"*

## What makes me enjoy this?
*"I love to be organized, I like connecting with people"*

## What's it like when I'm doing this?
*"It's great to feel organized and it makes my heart sing when I'm chatting with people"*

## EXERCISE

At the end of each day answer
the questions at the top of
**pages 55, 56** and **57**. Think
about small things like having
a nice chat with the postman
as well as bigger things like
doing well at a job interview.

- **What did I do well today?**

| | |
|---|---|
| Monday | |
| Tuesday | |
| Wednesday | |
| Thursday | |
| Friday | |
| Saturday | |
| Sunday | |

- **What did I enjoy?**

Monday

Tuesday

Wednesday

Thursday

Friday

Saturday

Sunday

- **What gave me a buzz?**

Monday

Tuesday

Wednesday

Thursday

Friday

Saturday

Sunday

Write a list of all the things that
you love doing, are energized
by and are good at.

Now compare this list with the
list of strengths you came up with
on **page 27** when you did the
introductory strengths exercise.

Write your **top strengths** on
**pages 61** and **62**. Alongside each
one, write what it's like for you
when you're doing that activity or
expressing that aspect of yourself.

| My top strengths | What's it like when I'm using it/doing it? |
|---|---|
| *Example:* | |
| 1. "Connecting with people" | "A buzz, keeps me energized for days, makes me happy" |
| 2. "Coming up with new ideas" | "I can't sleep, I get so wired up in a positive way" |
| 3. "Having new experiences" | "Probably the most exciting aspect of my life" |
| 4. "Organizing" | "Makes me feel calm, in control, settled. |
| 5. "Determination" | "I feel revved up and energetic when I am going after something I really want, whether it's something small like tickets for a show or something bigger, like a new job. |

1

2

3

4

|  | **My top strengths** | **What's it like when I'm using it/doing it?** |
|---|---|---|
| 5 | | |
| 6 | | |
| 7 | | |
| 8 | | |
| 9 | | |
| 10 | | |

Remember, the key to knowing whether something is a strength or just something you're good at is to ask yourself *"does it energize me?"* If it does, it's a strength.

### Do all the strengths you've written in the table energize you?

If so, you've discovered the strengths that really are you. If you're not sure, go back to the 'what's it like' column. If you just 'like' or 'are good at something', it might be that you've learned to do it well but it's not a natural strength. Remember, the key word is '**energize**'. Think about what energizes you.

# HASSAN'S STORY

One of Hassan's strengths is persistence. He had to sort out a problem for a customer that involved contacting head office. He phoned several times, and he kept going until eventually he found a person in the head office who could help him. Another one of his strengths is kindness and generosity, so he really enjoyed keeping the customer informed and getting back to them with an answer. This all feels great to Hassan.

For someone whose strengths are not persistence, kindness and generosity, this whole situation would have felt like a real pain. Hassan didn't realize that these are strengths of his that make it relatively easy and enjoyable for him to tackle situations like this.

# HOW IS THIS WEEK'S INSIGHT GOING TO HELP YOU?

Once you know your strengths, you can use them more consciously and deliberately.

Our strengths are natural to us, so it's not hard to apply them. And you've probably got the point by now that when we use our strengths, it's energizing.

Here's a simple strategy that will help you use and develop your strengths in your everyday life:

1. **Awareness** – Knowing what your strengths are in the first place is the first step. As well as doing the exercises in this workbook, ask others who know you well for feedback on this, so that you uncover any hidden strengths. A good way is to tell the person you're doing a personal development programme and ask them if they could give you some examples of when they've seen you at your best and what strengths they think you were using.

2. **Application** – Think about where you are applying your strengths in your life and how often. Ask yourself whether you could be using them more and in a greater number of situations. Just thinking about applying your strengths increases the likelihood that you will. Then you will feel more energized, which encourages you to do it all the more.

3. **Amplify** – Look at how and when you could increase your use of your strengths. We all get into the habit of doing the same things in the same way. Once you know your strengths, you can get more out of situations by amplifying them. For example, if you're a naturally good connector, make a conscious effort to connect with more people, even strangers on the way to work. Doing what you love puts a spring in your step. Doing it more and better means you're increasing the amount of time you feel energized.

4. **Add to** – Our strengths are the 'raw material' that make us who we are. To really excel, we need to have knowledge and skills, too. Think about what knowledge and skills you can learn or develop that will add power to your natural strengths. For example, if you love leading other people but you've never learned how to coach, learn some coaching skills. This will make the impact of your 'love to lead' strength much greater.

# TIP

If you're feeling fed up or flat, do
something that you know gives
you a little lift or a buzz. This
is one way that knowing your
strengths can help you.

# MOTIVATIONS

"TO SUCCEED IN THIS NEW WORLD, WE WILL HAVE TO LEARN, FIRST, WHO WE ARE."

PETER F. DRUCKER

# MOTIVATIONS

Our motivations are the reasons behind our actions. We tend not to think about our motivations, as they are intrinsically part of who we are.

Not everyone is motivated by the same things.

This week's exercises will help you identify your deepest motivations. Our motivations are also our strengths, so you may find that some of these came up last week.

( 1 )

At the beginning of this
week, look at the following
list and circle those that
apply to you.

## Power

you like to have responsibility
for people or tasks

•

## Ethics

you like to work in accordance
with certain morals

•

## Teamwork

you love to work with others

•

## Security

you want to feel secure
in your job or work

## Recognition

you like to be acknowledged by others
for your skills, effort and achievements

•

## Status

you like other people to
recognize your importance

•

## Activity

you like being busy and having a lot to do

•

## Freedom

you like to have autonomy
to work in the way you choose

•

## Competition

you like to compete with others

# Learning

you want experiences that
enable you to grow

•

# Leading

you love to be in charge

•

# Achievement

you like to have testing objectives
and challenges

•

# Friendship

you like to have close relationships

•

# Flexibility

you like to be able to choose
how you work

**EXERCISE**

In the following table, make
a note of the things that
motivated you each day.

## • What motivated me today?

| | |
|---|---|
| **Monday** | *Example: "Teamwork – weekly meeting with the team motivated me to help a couple of my colleagues, as it's important to me to be helpful"* |
| **Tuesday** | *"Power – I am responsible for an event next month. Having that responsibility is very motivating for me as I start arranging things"* |
| **Wednesday** | *"Activity – still working on the event and feeling very energized and motivated by it"* |
| **Thursday** | *"Leading – led a workshop today and remembered how much I love to lead"* |
| **Friday** | *"Recognition – I've done a great job this week and want this to be recognized at our team meeting on Monday"* |
| **Saturday** | *"Friendship – catching up with friends"* |
| **Sunday** | *"Security – checking my bank statements"* |

**EXERCISE**

## End-of-week reflection:

Write down the things that
motivated you the most and
are important for you to feel
fulfilled in your life.

You will never do something wholeheartedly unless you really want to do it. Motivation is crucial for the things that we really want to do. That's why it's important to understand what motivates you and it's why your motivations are also your strengths. For example, if you're motivated in a career where you are competing with others, such as a sales role, then you're much more likely to enjoy and be good at it than if you're not motivated by competition.

# JUDE'S STORY

Jude took a job at a not-for-profit organization whose purpose she really believed in. The ethical nature of the work really motivated and appealed to her. However, it didn't take her long to realize she felt restricted by the working practices. There were a lot of rules and protocols that had to be followed.

One of Jude's deeper motivations is being autonomous and flexible. She struggled in this job because the environment clashed so strongly with these deeper motivations and she felt stifled. She realized that some people love working within a certain set of rules and ways of doing things, but she just isn't like that. She made sure her next job gave her a lot more autonomy!

# HOW IS THIS WEEK'S INSIGHT GOING TO HELP YOU?

Quite simply, it means you can clearly decide what you want to do and what you don't want to do. Doing the things that motivate you will energize you, and you are more likely to succeed at them.

Sometimes, we all have to do some things that we don't want to do. But knowing what motivates you and what doesn't, can help you to:

**(a)** understand why you might be feeling less than positive about doing some things;

**(b)** ensure that you don't spend too much time doing things that are not motivating and may drag you down. We all have to do things that don't motivate us sometimes; that's to be expected. But if we're spending too much of our time on demotivating activities, it will lead to stress and unhappiness;

**(c)** make good career and work decisions. For example, if, like Jude in the earlier example, you're a person who is motivated by freedom, working in a strongly rules-based organization won't be the best fit for you.

# TIP

If you're asked to do a
particular job or project,
before you accept it, think
about whether it will actually
be motivating for you.

**WEEK 4**

# VALUES

"WORKING HARD FOR SOMETHING WE DON'T CARE ABOUT IS CALLED STRESS. WORKING HARD FOR SOMETHING WE LOVE IS CALLED PASSION."

SIMON SINEK

# VALUES

The things that matter to us (or our values) are the things that we would get upset or angry about if they were taken away. For example, justice is a value. If you get angry when you hear about incidences of injustice, then it's likely that this is an important value to you. We need to be doing things and being with people who align with our values if we're to feel comfortable and fulfilled.

Our values are also our strengths, because they are the things we really care about and tend to do whole-heartedly. For example, if one of your values is fairness and you're a police officer, then it's likely that you will carry out your work in an unbiased way.

As you work through the exercises this week, you might find that the values that you discover also came up in the strengths exercise in **Week 2**. That's because our values are also our strengths. Don't worry about the labels, though. What matters is that you discover the aspects of you that feel like the real you, irrespective of which section of this workbook they come up in.

## EXERCISE

At the start of the week,
look at the following list of
values and circle those you
think best represent you.

Feel free to add to the list.

**Making a difference**

**Doing the right thing**

**Fairness**

**Equality**

**Reliability**

**Loyalty**

**Honesty**

**Independence**

**Order**


**Courage**


**Freedom**


**Truth**


. . .


. . .


. . .


. . .

## EXERCISE

$$\left(2\right)$$

Throughout the week,
complete the following
tables on a daily basis.

## • What do I want to achieve?

*Example: "Finish my client proposal"*

Monday

Tuesday

Wednesday

Thursday

Friday

Saturday

Sunday

- **Why do I want to achieve this?**

  *"Because I promised I would and I want to get the business"*

| | |
|---|---|
| Monday | |
| Tuesday | |
| Wednesday | |
| Thursday | |
| Friday | |
| Saturday | |
| Sunday | |

- **Which of my values was I living by working toward what I wanted to achieve?**

*"Reliability – because I promised the proposal"*
*"Independence – because if I carry on winning business I can continue to work for myself"*

| | |
|---|---|
| Monday | |
| Tuesday | |
| Wednesday | |
| Thursday | |
| Friday | |
| Saturday | |
| Sunday | |

$$\left(3\right)$$

**End-of-week reflection:**
Think about and answer
the following questions.

- **Which of my values did I live this week?**

- **What were the circumstances, and what was it like, when I was expressing my values this week?**

- **Was this a typical week for me? If not, which of my other values do I get to express most weeks?**

- **How do my values influence the way I live my life?**

- **What impact do I have on others because of my values?**

# JOHN'S STORY

John had the chance to work on a new team
at an architectural practice. On his first day, he
had a meeting with the head of the practice,
who talked about how they all try to use the
notion of impeccability in everything they do.
That was evident in the décor, the quality of the
coffee, the way people presented themselves
and the way they spoke to their clients.

One of John's values is excellence, and he
would get inspired when he encountered
companies that seemed to pay attention to
all the little details. He would get annoyed
with people who he felt were slapdash or who
gave up at the first hurdle. The idea of working
with people whose attitude was about making
everything you did as good as possible was
really appealing, as it aligned so well with his
own value of excellence.

# HOW IS THIS WEEK'S INSIGHT GOING TO HELP YOU?

Knowing our values helps us realize why we can get so angry or upset sometimes. If something happens that conflicts with our values, it can be upsetting. Perhaps one of yours is high standards and someone you're working with is sloppy, or you're generous and you have a friend who is mean, or perhaps you really value honesty and you find out someone has lied to you. When you're clear about your values, it makes sense why some things push your buttons.

On the positive side, knowing our values helps us to be discriminating about who or what we spend our time on. Why spend time on things that clash with your values when you don't have to, and you know it will annoy or upset you?

# TIP

If you're not sure of your values,
think about what bothers you,
as these are the things that
go against your values. For
example, if it really bothers you
when people don't pay their way,
perhaps two of your values are
fairness and generosity.

# NOTES

**WEEK 5**

# STRENGTHS
# ON OVERDRIVE

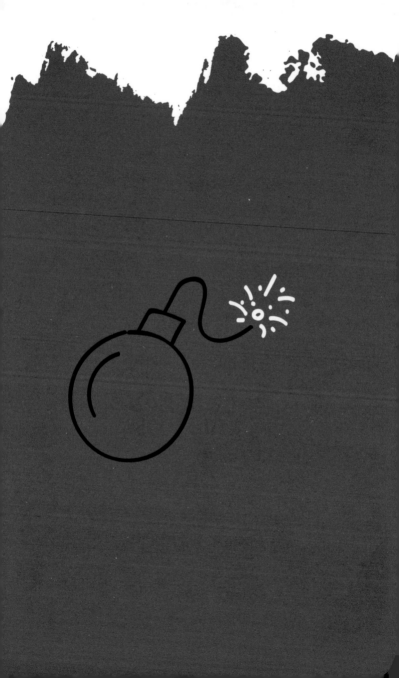

"AN UNEXAMINED
LIFE IS NOT
WORTH LIVING."

SOCRATES

# STRENGTHS ON OVERDRIVE

Our strengths are our greatest assets. However, sometimes they can become a problem if we overdo them. For example, someone who is great at analysing situations might sometimes overanalyse, resulting in others feeling that they are picking things apart too much. This can come across as being overly negative.

This week, we'll take a look at which of your strengths you might sometimes overdo. It's useful to know so that you keep your strengths in the 'sweet spot' and can avoid the negative consequences of overplaying them.

## EXERCISE

### 1

Look back at your strengths, motivations and values from the exercises in **Weeks 2**, **3** and **4**.

Think about whether you sometimes overdo these in a way that has a negative impact on yourself or other people.

| Strength (including motivations and values) | What can happen when I overdo this strength? |
|---|---|
| *Examples:* | |
| *Honesty* | *Bluntness when you're a bit too honest!* |
| *Drive* | *Other people sometimes feel you're overbearing because you can push too hard to get things done* |
| *Getting things done* | *Sometimes you get things done at the expense of doing them well* |
| *Conscientious* | *Maybe you're prone to perfectionism or not knowing when to stop* |
| *Love to be in charge* | *Perhaps you can become bossy or dominant* |
| *Optimistic* | *Sometimes your optimism might tip over into the realms of the unrealistic* |
| *Caring* | *Perhaps you sometimes care too much and become a bit suffocating* |

| Strength (including motivations and values) | What can happen when I overdo this strength? |
| --- | --- |
| | |
| | |
| | |
| | |

| Strength (including motivations and values) | What can happen when I overdo this strength? |
| --- | --- |
| | |
| | |
| | |
| | |

**EXERCISE**

Throughout the week, complete the following tables on a daily basis.

- **What goal do I want to achieve or what do I want to focus on?**

| | |
|---|---|
| Monday | |
| Tuesday | |
| Wednesday | |
| Thursday | |
| Friday | |
| Saturday | |
| Sunday | |

- **Which of my strengths will help me?**

| | |
|---|---|
| Monday | |
| Tuesday | |
| Wednesday | |
| Thursday | |
| Friday | |
| Saturday | |
| Sunday | |

- **Do I sometimes overdo this strength and, if so, what happens?**

Monday

Tuesday

Wednesday

Thursday

Friday

Saturday

Sunday

**EXERCISE**

**End-of-week reflection:**
Think about and answer
the following questions.

- **Were there times when I overdid any of my strengths this week?**




- **What was the effect on other people, myself or the task I was doing?**

- **How can I avoid this happening too much in the future?**

# EMMA'S STORY

Emma loves to be in charge and is a leader who people want to follow, because she has a really clear vision. One of her values is to make a difference. Her team is very loyal and supportive because they want to be part of the difference she is trying to make. Occasionally, however, particularly when she's feeling stressed, she becomes domineering. This is her strength of 'loving to be in charge' going into overdrive.

Emma and her team have all identified their strengths, and so it's easy for them to talk about their own and each others' strengths. When Emma goes into overly-dominant mode, they feel they can tell her. It doesn't come across as criticism, because they are talking about a strength that just needs to be pulled back into its positive zone.

# HOW IS THIS WEEK'S INSIGHT GOING TO HELP YOU?

Overdoing strengths is one of the most common de-railers of our success and effectiveness. That's why it's really important to know where you sometimes overdo yours.

A common situation that leads us to overdo our strengths is when we're under stress. For example, if one of your strengths is openness and honesty and you're feeling under pressure, you might blurt something out in a way that is too blunt and hurts someone's feelings.

Now that you've worked through the exercises this week and know which strengths you sometimes overdo, you can mitigate the potential negative impact by doing the following:

- Inform colleagues about the strengths you can overdo. For example, if you're giving someone feedback, start off by saying you want to be honest and invite the person to tell you if it comes over as a bit too blunt. That makes it easier for them to tell you because instead of it appearing as a criticism, they're actually telling you that you're overdoing a strength, which feels much less harsh.

- Discuss your strengths (yours and theirs), and how you might overdo them, with colleagues and friends. This gives you all permission to mention it in a constructive way if one of you starts overplaying your strengths. For example, it's relatively easy to say to someone *"you might be overplaying your connecting strength"* when a colleague is late for meetings because they can't pull themselves away from others who want to keep them talking. It would feel more critical to say *"you're late again because you stay around talking"*.

- Finally, knowing how you can overdo your strengths means you are more aware and so can catch yourself in the act, so to speak, and correct yourself, so that you are as effective as possible for as much of the time as possible.

# TIP

You can tell colleagues or friends that you can sometimes overdo a particular strength, so that they understand what you're about and don't perceive it as negative (e.g. if you're a very conscientious person who at times overdoes it and obsesses too much over the detail, tell them that).

This way they will understand that your intention is not negative, and it will also be easier for them to mention it to you so that you can rein it in.

# NOTES

**WEEK 6**

# WEAKNESSES

"IF YOU HEAR A
VOICE WITHIN YOU
SAY 'YOU CANNOT
PAINT', THEN BY ALL
MEANS PAINT, AND
THAT VOICE WILL
BE SILENCED."

VINCENT VAN GOGH

# WEAKNESSES

It might seem strange to be talking about weaknesses here when the route to a fulfilling life is to understand and play to our strengths. However, it's important to look at weaknesses, because we can tend to fixate too much on them, which can hold us back and knock our confidence.

We're all human and we all have weaknesses. There's nothing to be ashamed of. What we need to do is accept them and then decide whether or not we want to do anything about them.

It's helpful to split weaknesses into two categories: those that matter and those that don't. Many of our weaknesses are irrelevant, because they don't get in the way of our performance or fulfilment. For example, if you're a waiter and you're not very good at data analysis, it most probably doesn't matter in that job.

This week, we're going to take a look at weaknesses so that you can figure out which ones matter in relation to your current job or situation. It's important to note that we need to focus on our strengths in order to be happy or fulfilled, so I am not encouraging you to dwell on your weaknesses.

These exercises are intended to help you to do the opposite, i.e. *not* dwell on those weaknesses that don't matter and to find productive ways of mitigating those that do.

**EXERCISE**

At the beginning of the week, list your main weaknesses in the following table and how they matter in the context of your current work, studies or relationships. Then write some ideas on how you might mitigate the ones that matter.

Spend no longer than five minutes on this exercise.

| Weakness | How it impacts my work/studies/ relationships | How could I mitigate the weakness? |
|---|---|---|
| *Example:*<br>*Don't pay enough attention to detail sometimes* | *At work I often make needless errors which affect my colleagues because they spend their time correcting my mistakes* | *Allow myself more time double-checking my work*<br><br>*Ask a colleague to check work that's particularly important* |
| | | |
| | | |
| | | |

| Weakness | How it impacts my work/studies/relationships | How could I mitigate the weakness? |
| --- | --- | --- |
| | | |
| | | |
| | | |
| | | |

| Weakness | How it impacts my work/studies/relationships | How could I mitigate the weakness? |
| --- | --- | --- |
| | | |
| | | |
| | | |
| | | |

## EXERCISE

Throughout the week, think about
situations where you may have
to overcome a weakness.

How will you mitigate it, e.g. by
using a strength, by asking for
someone else's help, or simply by
being aware and taking extra care?

| | Situations where I may have to overcome a weakness | How will I mitigate it? |
|---|---|---|
| Monday | | |
| Tuesday | | |
| Wednesday | | |

|  | **Situations where I may have to overcome a weakness** | **How will I mitigate it?** |
|---|---|---|
| Thursday |  |  |
| Friday |  |  |

|  | **Situations where I may have to overcome a weakness** | **How will I mitigate it?** |
|---|---|---|
| Saturday |  |  |
| Sunday |  |  |

# MITIGATING WEAKNESSES

People sometimes think that there's nothing they can do about their weaknesses. Not true. There are five ways you can avoid being stymied by your weaknesses.

### 1. Use one of your strengths

If you know you're going to be in a situation where you might have to do something you're not very good at, think about whether one or more of your strengths can help you. For example, imagine you're attending a meeting where you don't know the people well and you think there may be conflict. If connecting with others is not a particular strength, you can't rely on that to build rapport. But, if you're a naturally curious person, you can use that curiosity to show that you are interested in their point of view. You could prepare a list of questions to show you want to know others' opinions.

### 2. Ask someone else to help

If you work with others, you'll have an idea of what they are good at and vice versa. Make a pact that you will help fill each other's gaps, if possible. For example, if you're not comfortable with analysing data and a colleague is, you could ask them to check your spreadsheets for you. And if you're good at written communications and they're not, you can offer to review important emails for them.

### 3. Break it down

We can sometimes think of what we perceive as our weaknesses as big things, and this kind of thinking can hold us back. For example, we might say we are 'shy' or 'a workaholic' or 'talk too much'. If you find yourself doing this, try to break this perceived weakness into component parts. Let's take shyness as an example. Ask yourself:

- Are there certain circumstances when I'm shy and others when I'm not?
- If the answer is 'yes', what enables me not to be so shy on some occasions?
- Could any of my strengths, values or motivations help me overcome my shyness?
- Is there a positive narrative I could adopt that would make me feel better about my shyness?

In this example, the answers might be something along these lines:

- I tend to be shyer when I'm meeting new people or in larger groups
- I tend to be less shy when I know people, or I think they like me
- My conscientiousness and desire to do a good job can help me, because I can only do a good job if I can put my shyness to one side sometimes and take the initiative with people
- I could try replacing the word 'shy' with 'understated'. And I could reframe my shyness and instead think of myself as the sort of person that caring, sensitive people value because they too see themselves as shy

## 4. Reframe it

The last point in number three on page 141 is an example of reframing. It can be very helpful as a way of thinking about something differently and in a way that is more constructive for us.

We can sometimes create a 'story' of ourselves that isn't very helpful when it comes to achieving what we want or feeling good about ourselves. For example, one executive always told himself he hated public speaking. Certainly, he didn't like to be in the spotlight and so he avoided having to talk to large groups whenever he could. However, this completely changed when he discovered his strengths, motivations and values. He realized that making a difference was really important to him and if he was able to speak to large numbers of people, it would help him make more of a difference. This realization didn't make him suddenly love public speaking, but it *made him want to do it!* He had some coaching in presentation skills that gave him some useful tips and techniques, and actually he turned out to be quite good, because people could see his passion for his subject and found him engaging.

If you think you have a particular weakness, ask yourself whether it's something you would like to be good at and, if so, think about which of your strengths, values and motivations might give you the fuel you need to do it anyway.

## 5. Be aware

The last thing you can do is simply be aware of when you're in a situation that requires you to use something that is a weakness. Sometimes this can't be avoided and acknowledging to yourself that you're going against your grain can mean you're less likely to give yourself a hard time and more likely to accept that you're just human after all. If that is hard, think about how you would treat your best friend if they had that same weakness. We can be much more forgiving of other people's weaknesses than we are of our own.

**End-of-week reflection:**
Think about and answer
the following questions.

- **What did I learn this week about my weaknesses?**

- **What is their potential impact?**

- **What might I do to mitigate them?**

# AMANDA'S STORY

Amanda is not good at reading other people. This usually doesn't matter in her work, because she's an administrator in a bookshop, which means she does the ordering, invoicing and returns. However, it does matter when her colleagues on the shop floor are very busy with customers, and she asks them for things that they haven't got time to do. She doesn't notice when they are looking stressed or run off their feet.

Now that she realizes this can be a problem, she asks the store manager whether it's a good time to go out onto the shop floor to speak to her colleagues, or whether she should wait. The team has also done a team strengths session, so it is much easier to say in a jokey way something such as, "Not now, Amanda, it's not a good time, but I'll come and find you when it is".

## HOW IS THIS WEEK'S INSIGHT GOING TO HELP YOU?

I sincerely hope that it will make you be more understanding of yourself and realize you're only human. We all have weaknesses and putting too much energy into trying to fix them is counterproductive.

Secondly, after this week's reflection, you should have some clear ideas about how you might mitigate any of your weaknesses – the ones that do matter – in particular situations.

# TIP

Instead of feeling that your weaknesses are a big problem, switch your thinking to see them as part of what it means to be human. Accept them and think about them in terms of how you can minimize the impact of them on you and what you want to achieve.

# NOTES

# INFLUENCES

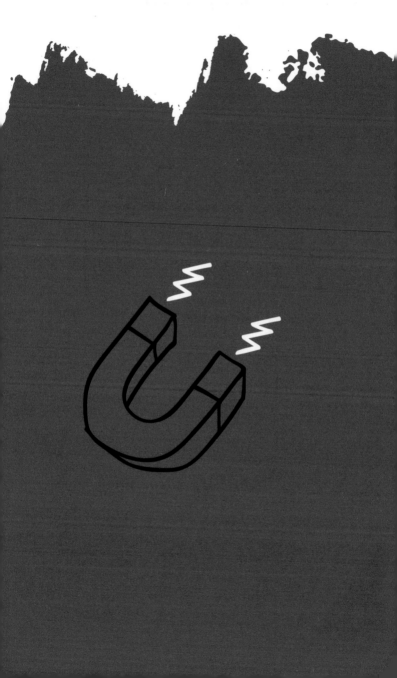

"YOU HAVE POWER
OVER YOUR MIND,
NOT OUTSIDE
EVENTS. REALIZE
THIS, AND YOU WILL
FIND STRENGTH."

**MARCUS AURELIUS**

# INFLUENCES

So far, we've looked at you and what kind of person you are – your strengths, values, motivations, overdone strengths and weaknesses. There is another factor that is important for our wellbeing and that helps us not to get knocked off balance too much. It's the way we approach things we can influence and things we can't.

In any given situation, there are some things we can control and some things we can't. The important thing is to identify what you can and can't influence, and only put effort into the former. Sometimes we stress ourselves out trying to change a situation that is simply beyond our sphere of influence. This can be frustrating and can have a negative effect on how we feel and perform. That's why this is an important area to look at.

This week we're going to look at identifying where you can or can't influence situations, so that you can direct your energy productively. This will help you avoid becoming frustrated by and wasting energy on situations that you can't influence.

## EXERCISE

In the following table, you'll find a list of hypothetical situations. Think about whether it's possible for you to have influence over each of these situations. If it's something you can influence, what could you do about it? The first row contains an example.

| Situations | Can I influence this or not? | What can I do to resolve the situation? |
| --- | --- | --- |
| | *Example: Usually, yes* | *I can't influence the bus running late today, but I can call my manager to let them know I'll be late. In future I can leave my house earlier so I can catch an earlier bus and make sure I'm never late* |
| Being late for work | | |
| Colleagues chatting too loudly | | |

| Situations | Can I influence this or not? | What can I do to resolve the situation? |
| --- | --- | --- |
| Getting angry about being stuck in a traffic jam | | |
| The price of groceries keeps rising | | |

| Situations | Can I influence this or not? | What can I do to resolve the situation? |
| --- | --- | --- |
| The head of your team made a decision that you do not agree with | | |

## EXERCISE

Throughout the week, make a note of any situations that you found frustrating or annoying. Think about whether you had any control over the situation, could have influenced the situation, or could have definitely done something about it (even if it's just to change your attitude toward it).

**Note:** You may find that nothing frustrates or annoys you on some days – that's great!

| | Frustrating or annoying situations | Did I have any control over the situation? | Could I have influenced the situation? | Could I have definitely done something about it? |
|---|---|---|---|---|
| Monday | | | | |
| Tuesday | | | | |
| Wednesday | | | | |

| | Frustrating or annoying situations | Did I have any control over the situation? | Could I have influenced the situation? | Could I have definitely done something about it? |
|---|---|---|---|---|
| Thursday | | | | |
| Friday | | | | |

| | Frustrating or annoying situations | Did I have any control over the situation? | Could I have influenced the situation? | Could I have definitely done something about it? |
|---|---|---|---|---|
| Saturday | | | | |
| Sunday | | | | |

$$\textbf{3}$$

**End-of-week reflection:**
Think about and answer
the following questions.

- **What things that occur quite frequently in my life/
work have I realized I can't influence?**

- **And what things can I influence?**

- **What action will I take in the future in regard to those things?**

# EMILY'S STORY

Emily was struggling with her boss. Some days he was quite reasonable and supportive. On other days, he was distant and frequently changed his mind about what he wanted. She never knew where she was with him, and it was starting to affect her badly. She realized that it was unlikely she could get him to change his behaviour, so she decided to adopt an attitude of 'oh, that's him and he's not likely to change'.

Changing her attitude meant she became less wound up by him. She also started looking for another job, which meant she was taking control rather than putting up with a situation that was unlikely to get any better.

# HOW IS THIS WEEK'S INSIGHT GOING TO HELP YOU?

If you spend time on something you have no control over, or worry about it, it's a waste of energy and can have a negative effect on everyday life. So, take the simple step of asking yourself whether a situation or problem is:

**(a)** something you can influence fully;

**(b)** something you can partly influence, or;

**(c)** something about which you can have no influence over whatsoever, which means that you can either stop giving yourself the stress of trying to sort the issue out and/or change your attitude toward it.

The point is that we waste energy worrying about things we have little or no control over. It's empowering and makes us more productive if we focus on the things we can actually influence.

# TIP

Sometimes our strengths, values and motivations can help us in situations where we feel we have no influence. For example, if you're an optimistic person, you can think about the positive elements of a situation. If you're a person who loves to make a difference, you can decide you will put your energies elsewhere. Keep going back to your list of strengths and see how they can help you.

# NOTES

**WEEK 8**

# BRINGING
# IT ALL
# TOGETHER

"IT IS NEVER
TOO LATE TO BE
WHAT YOU MIGHT
HAVE BEEN."

GEORGE ELIOT

This week you'll have a chance to collect all your insight into one place so that a summary of everything you've discovered about yourself - your **Strengths Profile** - can be viewed at a glance.

You'll also have the chance to practise a simple way of using your strengths in your daily life so that you live a more fulfilled and successful life.

# YOUR STRENGTHS PROFILE

Make a note of what you have learned over the course of this eight-week programme. Use the following pages and questions to transfer and keep a summary of the insights from each week's exercises.

# WEEK 1
**What are some of my proudest moments and what did I learn about myself from reflecting on them?**

# WEEK 2
**What are my key strengths?**

# WEEK 3
**What motivates me?**

## WEEK 4
**What are my values?**

---

## WEEK 5
**Which of my strengths do I sometimes overdo?**

---

## WEEK 6
**What are my weaknesses that matter and what are the main ways I can mitigate them?**

## WEEK 7
**Which frustrating situations do I now know I can't control, and how am I going to handle them in the future?**

## WEEK 8
**How can I use my strengths more often and effectively in the future?**

"SWITCH YOUR FOCUS TO THE THINGS YOU LOVE, THE THINGS THAT EXCITE YOU, AND THEN YOU'LL BE ON TRACK TO A REALLY GOOD LIFE."

RHONDA BYRNE

# BRINGING IT
# ALL TOGETHER

This week's exercises are designed to get you into the
habit of consciously using your strengths in everyday
life. If you can do this, you will be more fulfilled
more of the time.

## EXERCISE

At the beginning of the week, make a list of the main things you want to achieve or get done this week and how your strengths will help you to do it.

Remember that your motivations and values from **Weeks 3** and **4** are also your strengths.

|  | **How did I consciously use my strengths, values or motivations today?** | **What did I love doing and/or what energized me today?** |
|---|---|---|
| Monday | | |
| Tuesday | | |
| Wednesday | | |

Thursday

Friday

Saturday

Sunday

$$\left( 2 \right)$$

**End-of-week reflection:**
Think about and answer
the following questions.

- **When and how did I use my strengths, values and motivations this week?**

- **What was that like?**

- **How can I use my strengths, values and motivations more often and effectively in the future?**

# SALMA'S STORY

Salma had to ring a customer who had emailed her with a serious complaint. Some of her strengths are problem solving, connecting and data analysis. She knew she would need to win the trust of the customer and listen. She made sure that she allowed enough time for the call so she could connect by asking questions to show she cared, and she only moved into problem-solving mode when she had allowed the customer to vent.

It energized her to know that she had carefully thought through her approach, consciously using her strengths, and the customer felt heard.

# TIP

Take a few minutes at the beginning of each week to think about the most important things you have to do in the coming week. Then think about which of your strengths you can consciously and deliberately use to help you.

# REFLECTING
# ON YOUR
# DISCOVERIES

"THE MOST POWERFUL WEAPON ON EARTH IS THE HUMAN SOUL ON FIRE."

FERDINAND FOCH

Knowing your strengths, values and motivations is powerful. You can never reach your full potential or be fulfilled by trying to fix your weaknesses, but you can by knowing your strengths and stretching yourself in the direction of your strengths.

Over the past eight weeks, you've worked on identifying and developing your strengths, values and motivations. You've looked at how you might be tripped up by your weaknesses or overdoing your strengths, and you've considered some ways around those situations. Whether you are looking to find the right career path, course of study or just a better way to live and thrive, *The Strengths Workbook* has supplied you with the tools to help you.

You can work through the programme more than once with different projects, situations or goals in mind.

Have a think about the last
eight weeks of working through
*The Strengths Workbook*.

- **What has the experience been like?**

- **How has it helped me?**

- **What differences will the insights I've gained make to my life?**

# ABOUT THE AUTHOR

**Sally Bibb** is a leading figure in The Strengths Revolution and founder of Engaging Minds, a strengths consultancy that has achieved outstanding results for many well-known organizations including the AA, Cunard, EY, the NHS, Olympics, Saga and Starbucks.

Sally has worked all over the world, working with organizations to help them introduce strengths-based approaches to recruitment and development. Before setting up Engaging Minds she was a director at *The Economist* magazine.

She has an MSc in Change Agent Skills and Strategies from the University of Surrey and is a Fellow of the Royal Society of Arts.

Sally is an award-winning author of eight books, including *The Strengths Book: Discover How to Be Fulfilled in Your Work and in Life*.

www.sallybibb.com

www.engagingminds.co.uk

in @sallybibb

f @sallybibbauthorpage

🐦 @sallybibb

📷 @sallybibbauthor

# BY THE SAME AUTHOR

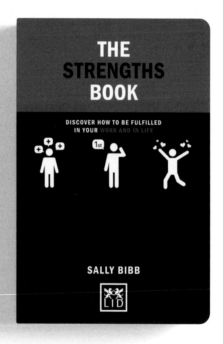

£9.99/$14.95
**conciseadvicelab.com**